Life Hack

The Ultimate Guide to Social Media Management

Copyright

Life Hack: The Ultimate Guide to Social Media Management
Kenneth Spresley

Self-publishing
contact@kennethactsout.com

ISBN: 979-8-3485-8347-7
Printed in the United States of America

Life Hack

The Ultimate Guide to Social Media Management

KENNETH SPRESLEY

To my family, your love and support make everything possible.
And to my mentors, thank you for your guidance and inspiration along this journey.

Acknowledgements

Over the course of my life, I owe a great deal of gratitude to the people who have helped shape me into the person I am today — far more than I could ever capture in a book. So, while I can only scratch the surface, I'd like to mention a few individuals who have been particularly influential.

First, I want to acknowledge my wife, Faith, and my children, Christian, Safia, and Samia. They are often the ones who bear the brunt of my crazy ideas and bear the greatest toll as I pursue these big goals — from filming a documentary on HOAs to creating a Christian hip-hop album, and yes, even writing this book. It's because of their love, support, and understanding that I am able to create freely and without hesitation.

Next, I want to express my deepest thanks to my mother, who has been an unwavering, day-one supporter — literally since birth. Her wisdom and insight over the years have been invaluable, and she continues to inspire me and my family every day.

Finally, I want to thank all of my mentors and those who have been inspirational throughout my journey. I've had the privilege of being influenced by so many incredible people who have shaped me both inside and out. A few names that come to mind include: Keith Releford, Rob McDonald, Chad Carloss, Carolyn Behymer-Lavalais, David Huntley, Cheryl Polote-Williamson, Brandon Rasley, Sean (Epiphany) Morrow, Cynt Marshall, Pastor Vincent Parker, Lisa Mitchell-Kastner, Niki Evansingston, Pastor and Mrs. Kashaa, Jamal Perkins, Brandon Seay, and Roderick Wright.

I thank you all immensely for everything you have done!

Life Hack: The Ultimate Guide to Social Media Management

Introduction

It was in the summer of 2011 when my journey began with one of the largest telecommunications companies in the United States. This is where I witnessed firsthand how social media could be leveraged in unprecedented ways. During this time, this telecommunications company was a pioneer in the digital space, understanding the power of online communities before many others did. Since then, I have spent over 15 years refining my expertise, working with both for-profit and non-profit organizations to build impactful social media strategies and foster meaningful online engagement.

As a communications and marketing professional, I have had the privilege of working at the forefront of this evolving digital landscape. This nearly two-decade career has been met with successes and failures, which have been instrumental in the learning process. You, too, will find that this evolving ecosystem will continue to shift, change, and adjust as it advances, and as new generations use it to communicate and educate themselves on products, services, and brands.

In such a short amount of time, we have all witnessed how social media has revolutionized the way businesses and individuals connect with their audiences. It is no surprise that it is no longer just a tool for communication—it is a powerful driver of brand awareness, engagement, and business growth. I want to express, however, that social media is a tool, and should not be the only tool you use in your toolkit. However, when used well it will enhance customer engagement and your brand's notoriety.

Effective social media management requires strategy, creativity, and adaptability. This book will equip you with the knowledge, tools, and best practices to master social media management and leverage it to achieve your goals, and is designed to take you through every essential aspect of social media management, from understanding different platforms to crafting a winning strategy, curating platform-specific content, building an engaged community, analyzing performance metrics, leveraging paid advertising and influencer collaborations, utilizing automation tools, and handling crisis management. Whether you are a business owner, marketer, or content creator, this book will provide you with actionable insights to elevate your online presence and maximize your impact.

One important lesson to remember throughout this journey is that effective social media management is both an art and a science. It requires constant learning, testing, and refining; by embracing this mindset, you'll develop a social media toolkit tailored to your unique audience and goals. Let's dive in!

Chapter 1: Understanding Social Media Platforms

When I first started my career in marketing, it was completely accidental. It was the spring of my junior year in high school when I stumbled into the world of multi-level marketing—though not in the way many would think. No, I wasn't lured to a lunch meeting only to be pitched a pyramid scheme selling fitness supplements… that would come later.

Instead, I discovered multi-level marketing through hosting events. A group of five friends and I brainstormed ways to make money by hosting parties, researched costs for renting event spaces, and pooled our limited resources. Since we were too young to sign contracts, we enlisted the help of a 21-year-old friend who signed on our behalf. Once the space was secured, we hit the ground running, promoting our event throughout our school. Without access to fancy flyers or bulletin boards, we relied on a talented friend to draw invitations, which we copied onto colorful paper and handed out with the help of our peers. This grassroots effort paid off—our event was packed, and we earned back two to three times our initial investment.

Back then, social media didn't exist in the way it does today, but the fundamental marketing principles we applied are still crucial in today's digital landscape. The key to mastering social media lies in truly understanding the environment—knowing the platforms, the algorithms, and, most importantly, the people who use them.

Increasingly, social media has become an essential part of modern communication, connecting billions of people worldwide. From small businesses to global corporations, brands leverage social platforms to engage with customers, share their messages, and build loyal communities. However, not all platforms serve the same purpose, and understanding their strengths, demographics, and functionalities is key to selecting the right ones for your brand or business.

We will explore the major social media platforms, analyze their audiences, and help you determine which platforms align best with your goals.

Overview of Major Platforms

Each social media platform has its own strengths and is designed to cater to specific user behaviors and preferences. Here's a breakdown of the most widely used platforms and their unique characteristics:

Facebook

- **Users**: Over **3 billion** monthly active users (as of 2024).
- **Best For**: Brand awareness, community building, paid advertising, and long-form content.
- **Strengths**: Advanced ad targeting, Facebook Groups, live streaming, and detailed analytics.
- **Challenges**: Organic reach has declined over time, requiring brands to invest in ads to maximize visibility.

Instagram

- **Users**: Over **2 billion** monthly active users.
- **Best For**: Visual storytelling, brand aesthetics, influencer marketing, and product showcasing.
- **Strengths**: High engagement rates, Reels for short videos, shopping features, and influencer collaborations.
- **Challenges**: Competitive algorithm, requires consistent posting and high-quality visuals.

Twitter (Now X)

- **Users**: Around **500 million** monthly active users.
- **Best For**: Real-time updates, industry trends, customer service, and brand personality.
- **Strengths**: Hashtags for discoverability, fast-paced interaction, strong news and tech industry presence.
- **Challenges**: Limited character count, requires frequent posting, algorithm changes.

LinkedIn

- **Users**: Over **1 billion** professionals.
- **Best For**: B2B marketing, professional networking, thought leadership, and job recruitment.
- **Strengths**: Industry-specific content, lead generation for professionals, LinkedIn articles, and strong organic reach.
- **Challenges**: Requires professional and value-driven content, longer sales cycle for B2B marketing.

TikTok

- **Users**: Over **1.5 billion** monthly active users.
- **Best For**: Short-form video content, viral trends, and engaging younger audiences.
- **Strengths**: High engagement, discoverability through the For You Page (FYP), influencer potential.
- **Challenges**: Short content lifespan, unpredictable algorithm, high content creation demand.

Pinterest

- **Users**: Over **450 million** monthly active users.
- **Best For**: Inspiration-based marketing, e-commerce, lifestyle brands, and long-term content visibility.
- **Strengths**: Pins have a longer lifespan, strong referral traffic to websites, great for product discovery.
- **Challenges**: Slower audience growth, requires high-quality visuals, less interactive than other platforms.

Identifying the Right Platforms for Your Brand

Now that you've studied the strengths, challenges, and best use cases for each of these major platforms, you have to decide which platform is the best for your business. As you determine that, consider these factors:

- **Your Target Audience**: Where do they spend their time online?

- **Your Content Style**: Do you create videos, blogs, infographics, or photos?
- **Your Business Goals**: Are you focused on brand awareness, lead generation, or direct sales?
- **Industry Trends**: Which platforms are performing well in your industry?

For example, if you are in e-commerce, Instagram and Pinterest are excellent choices due to their visual nature. If you are in B2B marketing, LinkedIn and Twitter may be more effective.

Understanding Audience Demographics and Behavior

Each platform attracts a different audience. Here's a demographic breakdown to help you align your brand with the right social media users:

- **Facebook**: Most popular among users aged **25 to 55**. Strong presence in all demographics.
- **Instagram**: Heavily used by **18 to 35-year-olds**. Perfect for millennials and Gen Z.
- **Twitter**: Appeals to professionals, journalists, and tech-savvy individuals aged **18 to 45**.
- **LinkedIn**: Dominated by professionals aged **25 to 55**, great for career and business-related content.
- **TikTok**: Primarily **16 to 34-year-olds**, with a highly engaged younger audience.
- **Pinterest**: Popular with **25 to 50-year-old women**, ideal for lifestyle and home-related businesses.

Pro Tip: Analyzing platform insights and industry reports can help refine your audience strategy. Many businesses successfully use a mix of platforms to reach different segments of their target audience, and as I often stress with organizations building social media strategies, you will rarely need to be on all of these platforms. Start small and remain adaptable to trends that could suggest shifts in your target audience.

Understanding the different environments of social media is the first step in building an effective strategy. Each platform offers unique advantages, and the key is to align your brand's strengths with the right audience and content type. By choosing the right platforms and leveraging their features strategically, you can build an engaging and impactful online presence.

Once you've learned and identified your environments, then it's time to craft a powerful social media strategy—the foundation of successful social media management.

Chapter 1 Challenge

Now that you know a bit more about each platform—their strengths, challenges, and audience behaviors—write down which platform(s) would fit your business type and why:

Chapter 2: Creating a Social Media Strategy

If there is one thing that gets me out of bed, it's developing a solid strategy. Two years ago, my wife and I began planning my 40th birthday party. I knew I wanted it to be the biggest and best celebration I could throw for myself, and I also knew it wasn't going to plan itself. So, I started thinking about what I envisioned. I wanted an 80s-themed party—since I was born in the 80s—and I wanted my family and friends to fully embrace the era by arriving in 80s-themed costumes.

Bringing this vision to life required careful planning. I had to research outfits, design an invitation flyer, choose the right venue, curate an 80s-themed food and drink menu, and decide how far I was willing to commit to the theme.That last part? It meant making a bold choice—I would have to shave my beard. Surprising as it may seem, there weren't many men sporting full beards in the 80s. So, in the name of authenticity, I took the plunge and shaved it off.

The result? Many of my family and friends arrived at the party, greeted me, and had no idea who I was. With my full 80s outfit and missing beard, I was practically unrecognizable! But that night, something amazing happened—it became one of the most memorable celebrations I had ever experienced. Even my mother, who knew a thing or two about the 80s, had a blast.

That party was a success because of one thing: a well-thought-out strategy. It required time, resources, and, most importantly, clear goals. Without a plan, it would have been chaotic and far less impactful.

Just like planning an unforgettable event, an effective social media strategy is the foundation of success. Without a well-structured plan, businesses often waste time and resources on ineffective efforts. We're going to dive into the key steps to developing a results-driven social media strategy that ensures your efforts are not just seen—but truly make an impact.

Step One: Set Clear Goals

The key to creating an effective strategy is to first define clear objectives. Start with your **"why"** by asking:

- **Why do we need an online presence?**
- **Why should we choose this platform over another?**
- **What are we hoping to accomplish with this tool?**

Some common goals include:

- **Brand Awareness** – Expanding your audience and increasing recognition.
- **Engagement** – Fostering meaningful interactions with your followers.
- **Conversions** – Driving sales, sign-ups, or leads through strategic content.
- **Customer Service** – Using social media as a support channel to resolve issues efficiently.

As you begin answering these core questions, start building SMART (Specific, Measurable, Achievable, Relevant, Time-bound) goals. Setting SMART goals ensures clarity and focus in your strategy.

Step Two: Identify Your Target Audience & Craft Audience Personas

Understanding your audience is the foundation of crafting compelling content. While working for a large national medical association, we frequently discussed our target audience—our physician members. Identifying their demographics was straightforward: age, gender, location, income level, and of course, their profession. But understanding their psychographics—interests, values, and lifestyle—required deeper engagement.

The real challenge, however, was determining which social media platforms they were most likely to engage with us on. During my first few years in the role, I intensively studied their behaviors, observing where they posted the most, testing content across platforms, and analyzing engagement patterns. Through this process, I discovered that many physicians were highly active on Twitter (now X), using it for professional discussions and medical advancements, while others operated within the privacy of Facebook groups, engaging in closed-door conversations with their peers.

For businesses selling a general product, defining a target audience may be more complex. However, if you have a niche product, service, or customer type, identifying your audience can be much more straightforward.

When defining your target audience, consider these three key areas:

- **Demographics** – Age, gender, location, income level
- **Psychographics** – Interests, values, lifestyle, motivations
- **Social Media Behavior** – Platform preferences, engagement patterns, posting habits

Crafting detailed customer personas based on these factors will help you tailor your messaging and content strategy to resonate deeply with the right audience, ultimately increasing engagement and conversions.

Step Three: Develop a Content Calendar & Posting Schedule

Remember that medical association I mentioned in Step Two? Before I arrived, they had more of a "post as much as you can, as often as you can" approach to their social media strategy. While it seemed like they were being consistent, their content strategy lacked focus, leading to scattered messaging across different platforms.

Through continuous coaching, I helped them understand that each platform has a different algorithm and consistency requirement. To maximize engagement and attract new members, we actually had to reduce our content output and align with each platform's best practices.

Here's what that looked like:

- **Facebook**: 1-2 posts per day
- **Twitter (now X) & LinkedIn**: Up to 5 posts per day
- **Instagram**: Up to 7 posts per week

After 18 months, we refined our strategy and reduced posts by nearly 2,000 compared to previous years. Although we haven't yet covered social media analytics, here's what happened after implementing platform-specific consistency:

- **Engagement**: Grew by 47.3% (2.4M interactions)
- **Impressions**: Increased by 80.5% (45M views)
- **Post Link Clicks**: Jumped by 170% (1M clicks)
- **Audience Growth**: Expanded by 15.4% (15,030 new followers)
- **Video Views**: Soared by 740% (2.5M views)

Consistency is crucial for social media success—especially when aligned with each platform's unique algorithm. A well-planned content calendar helps keep you organized, ensures steady posting, and allows your social media efforts to align with marketing campaigns and trends.

In Chapter 7, we'll explore scheduling tools that can help streamline content management and improve efficiency. For now, just remember: consistency is key to an effective social media strategy.

Now that you have the steps for creating your social media strategy, let's talk about content and explore platforms that can help you create high-quality, engaging content tailored for different audiences.

Chapter 2 Challenge

After reading this chapter, write out five goals below, using SMART (Specific, Measurable, Achievable, Relevant, Time-bound) goals:

Goals:

1	
2	
3	
4	
5	

Chapter 3: Content Creation & Curation

We have arrived at one of my favorite topics—next to analytics and strategy—content creation. Creating compelling content is at the heart of any successful social media strategy. Content is what draws people in, fosters engagement, and helps build a brand's personality. Whether it's an eye-catching image, a thought-provoking blog post, or an entertaining video, high-quality content can make a brand stand out in an increasingly crowded digital ecosystem.

Social media platforms prioritize different types of content, so understanding how to craft and curate content that aligns with each platform's unique environment is essential for success. We're going to break down the various types of content used across social media platforms, best practices for creating engaging posts, top tools for graphic design and video editing, and the power of user-generated content. So, buckle up for a ride on the content train! Let's start with the types of content used across each social media platform.

Types of Content Used Across Social Media Platforms

Each social media platform thrives on specific types of content. While some focus heavily on visuals, others prioritize short-form text updates, discussions, or live interactions. Here's an overview of content types and where they perform best:

- **Images** – Instagram, Facebook, Pinterest, LinkedIn
    - High-quality photos and infographics grab attention and convey messages quickly.
- **Videos** – TikTok, Instagram (Reels), YouTube, Facebook
    - Short-form videos (TikTok, Reels, Shorts) are perfect for viral trends, while long-form videos (YouTube, Facebook) work well for in-depth storytelling.

- **Live Streams** – Facebook, Instagram, LinkedIn, YouTube
    - Live interactions allow brands to connect directly with audiences in real-time—ideal for Q&A sessions, product demos, and behind-the-scenes content.
- **Text-Based Posts** – Twitter, LinkedIn, Facebook
    - Thought leadership, industry news, and concise updates work well on platforms where users engage in discussions.
- **Stories (Temporary Content)** – Instagram, Facebook, Snapchat
    - Short-lived content creates urgency and encourages daily engagement.
- **Blog & Article Links** – LinkedIn, Facebook, Twitter
    - Sharing long-form content like blogs and articles helps establish expertise and drive traffic to websites.
- **Memes & GIFs** – Twitter, Instagram, Facebook
    - Entertaining and humorous content that resonates with audiences can go viral quickly.

Tips for High-Quality and Engaging Content

Your content must stand out, and to do that, it has to be high-quality and engaging. I know I may sound like a broken record here, but you must KNOW YOUR AUDIENCE. You need to understand their preferences, pain points, and interests to craft content they will find valuable.

Remember: You are competing with countless others for the same customer's attention, and you literally have seconds to make them stop scrolling. That brings us to one of the most critical elements: the hook.

What Is a Hook?

A hook is a compelling first line, image, or video clip designed to grab a person's attention immediately and encourage them to engage with your content. This may seem trivial, but many social media strategies fail at this step, crippling engagement from the start.

Examples of Hooks:

- *"I have a secret… [dramatic pause]"*
- *"You're making this HUGE mistake in your marketing!"*
- *"Your social media manager is trash, and here's why!"*

Okay, that last example might be a little harsh, but believe me—it works. Hooks must be compelling, and they have just 1-3 seconds to capture someone's attention.

When I worked for a company (which shall remain nameless), I learned something about human psychology: People lose interest fast. In fact, research has shown that the average human attention span is around 6 seconds—similar to a goldfish. This taught me that everything I create must instantly capture and hold attention.

Here are a few additional best practices for making your content stand out:

- **Use High-Resolution Media** – Poor-quality photos, videos, and graphics can diminish credibility.
- **Leverage Storytelling** – People connect emotionally with stories, making them more likely to engage.
- **Keep It Concise** – Short, impactful messaging is more likely to be absorbed and shared.
- **Include a Call-to-Action (CTA)** – Encourage users to engage by prompting likes, comments, shares, or clicks.
- **Optimize for Mobile** – Most users access social media via mobile devices, so ensure your content is mobile-friendly.
- **Stay Consistent** – Establish a recognizable brand voice and a steady posting schedule.

Although these best practices are tried and true, sometimes you may be able to get away on a best practice or two. For instance, sometimes people will overlook the quality of the video if it has a deep emotional connection. This has been the case in a few projects that I personally developed. One dealt with a physician's personal journey during the COVID pandemic and the other dealt with the personal affects of suicide. In both of those campaigns, I had very little control over the quality of the footage collected, however, the messages were so impactful that they pulled a natural engagement. This should be the standard, but if it's all you have make the message strong with your audience.

Best Tools for Graphic Design & Video Editing

As of the time I'm writing this book, I have not received any sponsorship deals from any of the tools listed. Also, the digital landscape changes rapidly, so some tools may evolve or be replaced over time. However, here are some of the tools I personally use or have used in the past:

Free or Affordable Tools:

- **GIMP** – A free, open-source tool for creating and editing graphics.
- **DaVinci Resolve** – A free yet powerful video editing software.
- **Canva** – A user-friendly tool for graphic design and social media posts.
- **CapCut** – Great for editing TikToks, YouTube Shorts, and Reels.

Premium Tools:

- **Adobe Photoshop** – Industry-standard tool for graphic design and image editing.
- **Final Cut Pro & Adobe Premiere Pro** – Used for high-quality video production.

User-Generated Content (UGC): What It Is & How to Leverage It

User-generated content (UGC) is content created by customers, fans, or followers that showcases your brand in an authentic way. It can be photos, videos, reviews, or testimonials shared on social media. UGC is powerful because it builds trust—people are more likely to trust content from peers than from branded advertisements.

Ways to Leverage UGC:

- **Encourage Customers to Share** – Create branded hashtags for users to tag their posts.
- **Feature UGC on Your Channels** – Showcase customer content on your official pages.
- **Run Contests & Challenges** – Incentivize followers to participate in hashtag challenges.
- **Engage with UGC** – Comment, like, and share user-generated posts to build community and increase brand loyalty.

By incorporating a mix of branded and user-generated content, brands can foster stronger relationships with their audience and enhance credibility.

With these insights, you're now equipped to create engaging, high-quality content that resonates with your audience. Next, we'll dive into engagement strategies and community-building techniques to ensure your content doesn't just exist—it thrives!

Chapter 4: Engagement & Community Building

Years ago, I was a communications and marketing director for a local church in the Dallas area. When I stepped into the role, I quickly realized that I had to build a social media strategy from scratch—from just a few scattered pieces, like trying to construct a house with nothing but a couple of 2x4s. The church had social media accounts, but no one was actively engaging with the people commenting, nor were they responding to direct messages. It was a blank canvas, and I saw an opportunity to lay a solid foundation for meaningful digital interactions.

I started with the basics—understanding the social media environment, improving response times, and acknowledging comments. These small but crucial steps led to gradual increases in engagement. But I knew we could do more.

As the strategy evolved, we began incorporating live streaming sessions where I engaged with viewers watching the streamed services online. In the comments, I would welcome people to the live stream, address their questions, ask them to share the video, and encourage discussions. This transformed our social media presence from passive to interactive, turning viewers into an engaged digital congregation. It reinforced something I've seen time and time again—engagement is the lifeblood of social media success.

Social media is designed to be a two-way street. Without engagement, even the most well-crafted content can fall flat. Businesses and brands that prioritize interaction build loyal communities, foster trust, and create deeper connections with their audience. In this chapter, we will explore why engagement matters, how to boost it, strategies for responding to comments and messages, and how to build thriving online communities that support long-term growth.

Importance of Engagement & How to Boost It

Social media platforms prioritize content that sparks interactions, meaning engagement directly affects visibility. A post with high engagement is more likely to appear in users' feeds, leading to greater reach and impact. Engagement is also a key indicator of a brand's relationship with its audience—it signals trust, authenticity, and connection.

To boost engagement:

- **Create Conversational Content** – Ask open-ended questions, encourage discussions, and invite opinions.
- **Use Engaging Visuals** – High-quality images, GIFs, and videos capture attention better than plain text.
- **Leverage Interactive Features** – Polls, quizzes, and "Ask Me Anything" (AMA) sessions encourage participation.
- **Post Consistently** – Regular, predictable posting helps maintain audience interest.
- **Respond Promptly** – Acknowledging comments and messages fosters two-way conversations.
- **Encourage User Participation** – UGC campaigns, contests, and challenges get followers involved.
- **Utilize Storytelling** – Authentic narratives resonate more than corporate-style updates.
- **Go Live** – Live streaming builds real-time engagement and deepens audience connection.
- **Collaborate with Influencers** – Partnering with influencers increases credibility and engagement.
- **Use Hashtags Strategically** – Relevant hashtags improve discoverability and boost interaction.

Strategies for Responding to Comments and Messages

For the sake of this discussion, this company will remain nameless. However, working for **this large-scale company** taught me that answering every message or comment was sometimes unrealistic, whether because of limited staff or limited impact on the brand's notoriety. In those instances, policies were created to focus on comments and messaging that had the greatest impact to the brand–usually determined by the number of followers the user had on their social media account. These days there are other reasons to avoid responding, which we will talk about later in chapter 8, however, for the sake of this chapter, here are a few ways you could respond effectively to positive or negative comments:

- **Be Prompt and Personable** – Quick responses show that you value your audience's input.
- **Acknowledge All Comments** – Even a simple "thank you" or emoji reaction can foster goodwill.
- **Encourage Further Interaction** – Ask follow-up questions to keep the conversation going.
- **Address Negative Comments with Care** – Maintain professionalism and offer solutions instead of being defensive.
- **Use a Consistent Brand Voice** – Whether casual or formal, ensure responses align with your brand personality.
- **Utilize Automation for FAQs** – Chatbots and saved responses can help manage inquiries efficiently.

A well-managed engagement strategy not only improves customer satisfaction but also strengthens brand loyalty.

Growing a Loyal Audience Through Authentic Interactions

One thing about loyalty, it is built over time through trust and genuine connection and sustaining loyalty involves a large amount of transparency. To foster audience loyalty, consider the following:

- **Show Behind-the-Scenes Content** – Transparency humanizes your brand and builds relatability.
- **Celebrate Your Audience** – Feature user stories, testimonials, or milestone shout-outs.
- **Offer Exclusive Content** – Provide special content for loyal followers (e.g., early access, giveaways).
- **Be Real & Vulnerable** – Authenticity breeds connection. Share challenges and real experiences.

- **Engage Beyond Promotion** – Talk about industry trends, social causes, and topics beyond your products.

Consistently engaging in meaningful ways turns casual followers into brand advocates who not only support your business but also encourage others to do the same.

Building & Managing Online Communities and Groups

A strong community fosters long-term engagement and brand loyalty. Here's how to build and manage one effectively:

- **Create a Purpose-Driven Community** – Define what your community stands for and what value it provides.
- **Choose the Right Platform** – Facebook Groups, Discord, LinkedIn Groups, and Reddit are great options.
- **Encourage Member Participation** – Pose discussion topics, host challenges, and invite user contributions.
- **Moderate Wisely** – Establish clear rules to keep the community respectful and engaging.
- **Recognize and Reward Active Members** – Give shout-outs, badges, or exclusive perks to top contributors.

A thriving online community not only strengthens engagement but also builds a network of brand advocates who drive organic growth.

Next, we will explore social media analytics and performance tracking—key elements in refining your strategy and maximizing your impact. Also, if you did not know, it's one of my favorite topics.

Chapter 5: Social Media Analytics & Performance Tracking

In the summer of 2016, I was given the task of increasing video views for a local church. At the time, the church was averaging about 2,750 views per month, but engagement was steadily declining. After conducting careful research, I discovered a key insight—many people simply wanted or needed prayer. This led me to pitch an idea to the lead pastor: a weekly video series called "Prayer Time."

The concept was simple, but it struck a chord. The video series quickly gained traction, and we saw its success unfold through performance tracking. Video views jumped over 300% in the final months of the year and resulted in a 423% increase in total video views compared to the previous year. This experience reinforced a critical lesson—tracking performance and making data-driven adjustments can significantly amplify social media impact.

Tracking the performance of your social media efforts is essential for long-term success. Without clear insights into what is working and what isn't, businesses can waste valuable time and resources on ineffective strategies. Social media analytics help measure progress, identify areas for improvement, and ensure that your efforts align with your business goals.

In this chapter, we will explore key performance indicators (KPIs) to monitor, the best analytics tools available, and how to adjust your strategy based on data insights. By the end, you'll have a roadmap for optimizing your social media presence through data-driven decision-making.

Key Performance Indicators (KPIs) to Monitor

Key Performance Indicators, or KPIs, measure the effectiveness of your social media strategy. It's crucial to track relevant KPIs to ensure you are landing on the right message with your audience. These metrics provide data-driven insights that help businesses refine their approach. Here are the most important KPIs to monitor:

- **Engagement Rate** – Measures likes, comments, shares, and interactions per post.
- **Reach & Impressions** – Reach refers to unique users who see your content, while impressions count total views.
- **Follower Growth** – Tracks how your audience is expanding over time.
- **Click-Through Rate (CTR)** – Measures how often users click on links in your posts or ads.
- **Conversion Rate** – Assesses how many social media users take a desired action, such as signing up for a newsletter or making a purchase.
- **Bounce Rate** – Analyzes how many users leave your website after clicking through from social media.
- **Response Rate & Time** – Monitors how quickly and effectively you respond to customer inquiries.
- **Share of Voice (SOV)** – Compares your brand's social media presence against competitors.

Understanding these KPIs will allow you to identify strengths and weaknesses in your strategy, ensuring a data-driven approach to social media success.

Analytics Tools

There are numerous analytics tools available to help track social media performance. Here are some options:

- **Google Analytics** – Tracks website traffic from social media, conversions, and audience behavior.
- **Facebook Insights** – Provides detailed data on post performance, audience demographics, and engagement.
- **Instagram Insights** – Shows follower growth, impressions, reach, and engagement metrics.
- **Twitter Analytics** – Monitors tweet engagement, impressions, follower trends, and click-through rates.
- **LinkedIn Analytics** – Tracks content performance, audience insights, and follower engagement.

- **Hootsuite Analytics** – Offers multi-platform tracking and customizable reports.
- **Sprout Social** – Delivers advanced analytics and reporting, including sentiment analysis.
- **Buffer Analytics** – Provides insights into post performance, scheduling, and engagement trends.

Each tool has its own strengths, and using a combination of them can provide a comprehensive view of your social media performance.

How to Adjust Strategy Based on Performance Data

Analyzing social media performance data is only valuable if you use it to improve your strategy. Here are some ways to make data-driven adjustments:

- **Identify High-Performing Content** – Determine which posts generate the most engagement and replicate their success by creating similar content.
- **Adjust Posting Frequency & Timing** – Use insights on when your audience is most active to optimize your posting schedule.
- **Refine Audience Targeting** – If engagement rates are low, reevaluate your audience demographics and tailor content to better match their interests.
- **Test Different Content Formats** – Experiment with videos, images, live streams, and interactive posts to see what resonates best with your audience.
- **Improve Call-to-Actions (CTAs)** – If your conversion rates are low, tweak your CTAs to be more compelling and action-driven.
- **Analyze Competitor Data** – Compare your performance with industry competitors. See what's working for your competitors and adopt successful strategies.
- **Reallocate Budget** – If paid campaigns aren't delivering results, adjust ad targeting, creatives, or budget allocation.
- **Engage More with Your Audience** – If response rates are low, focus on improving community interactions and customer service efforts.

By continually analyzing and adjusting your approach based on performance data, you can refine your social media strategy, improve engagement, and drive better business outcomes. Let me share a quick story from a content creator's perspective to illustrate this point.

As a Christian hip-hop artist, attracting people to my Instagram and Facebook pages was a struggle. I was throwing everything at the wall, hoping something would stick, but nothing seemed to work. Frustrated, I took a step back and began analyzing the Instagram pages of other successful Christian hip-hop artists. That's when I started noticing patterns and trends.

Some artists incorporated comedy into their posts to attract a specific audience, while others repeatedly posted short-form music videos to keep engagement high. I decided to mimic these strategies while adding my own unique style, and suddenly, I saw results—my followers began growing by an average of 20 new followers per day.

But I didn't stop there. I took my best-performing posts, invested in paid ads and boosted them, leading to even greater engagement and follower growth. I also realized that many of these artists collaborated with one another, introducing their audiences to each other. So, I started collaborating with them as well, which further expanded my reach and credibility.

This experience reinforced a valuable lesson: studying your analytics will help you refine your strategy and signal when it's time to pivot. Sometimes, the key to success isn't just what you post, but how you amplify it. By applying these insights, my Facebook following grew from 300 to thousands, and my Instagram following jumped from 500—resulting in a collective increase of 15,000 followers in just three months.

This brings us to the next powerful step in social media growth—paid advertising and influencer collaborations. If you want to maximize reach, accelerate growth, and tap into new audiences, understanding how to effectively leverage social media ads and influencer partnerships is crucial. Let’s dive into how these strategies can take your social media presence to the next level.

Chapter 6: Paid Advertising & Influencer Collaborations

While organic reach is essential for building a community, paid advertising and influencer collaborations offer powerful ways to expand your reach and achieve specific business goals.

I remember the first time I ran my own personal paid ad—it was intimidating. The technical jargon, the multiple options, and the pressure of not having a large budget made it seem overwhelming. However, I quickly realized that advertising is less complicated than it seems. Today, you can launch a paid campaign for as little as $20, and when done correctly, it can drive massive results—especially when you KNOW YOUR AUDIENCE.

I've personally spent as little as $30 on boosted ads that resulted in hundreds of thousands of views and high engagement. This success is largely due to social media platforms evolving into sophisticated advertising ecosystems that allow brands to target their audience with precision. If you don't know your audience well, Facebook and Instagram can even help by targeting similar personas to the ones who already follow and engage with your content.

Beyond paid ads, influencers have become some of the most trusted voices in marketing, introducing brands to highly engaged and loyal audiences. In this chapter, we will explore the fundamentals of paid social media advertising, how to set up effective ad campaigns, the benefits of influencer partnerships, and strategies for measuring return on investment (ROI).

Understanding Paid Ads on Different Platforms

Paid social media advertising allows businesses to amplify their reach and engagement by placing targeted ads in front of users who fit their ideal customer profile. Each platform offers unique advertising options:

- **Facebook & Instagram Ads** – Highly targeted ads based on demographics, interests, and behaviors. Options include carousel ads, video ads, and sponsored stories.
- **Twitter (now X) Ads** – Promoted tweets, trends, and accounts help brands increase visibility and drive engagement.
- **LinkedIn Ads** – Best for B2B marketing, featuring sponsored content, InMail, and dynamic ads for professional targeting.
- **TikTok Ads** – Focused on engaging video content, offering in-feed ads, branded hashtag challenges, and TopView placements.
- **Pinterest Ads** – Ideal for e-commerce and lifestyle brands, featuring promoted pins that blend seamlessly into organic content.
- **YouTube Ads** – Video-based advertising that reaches users before, during, or after videos with skippable and non-skippable formats.

Understanding each platform's strengths allows businesses to allocate their budget strategically, ensuring the best ROI for their campaigns.

Setting Up Effective Ad Campaigns

To maximize the impact of paid social media campaigns, follow these steps:

- **Define Clear Objectives** – Set specific goals such as increasing website traffic, generating leads, or boosting engagement.
- **Know Your Audience (I've said this before somewhere.)** – Utilize audience insights to refine targeting based on age, location, interests, and behaviors.
- **Choose the Right Ad Format** – Select from image ads, video ads, carousel ads, or interactive formats based on platform and objectives.
- **Craft Compelling Ad Copy** – Use concise and persuasive messaging with a strong call to action (CTA).

- **Design Visually Engaging Content** – High-quality images and videos increase engagement and conversion rates.
- **Set a Budget & Bidding Strategy** – Determine daily or lifetime budgets and choose between cost-per-click (CPC), cost-per-thousand-impressions (CPM), or cost-per-action (CPA) bidding models.
- **A/B Testing** – Run variations of ad creatives and copy to determine which performs best.
- **Monitor & Optimize** – Use real-time analytics to track performance and make necessary adjustments to improve results.

By following these steps, businesses can ensure their advertising dollars are spent effectively to drive meaningful results.

Partnering with Influencers to Expand Reach

Influencer marketing has become a powerful tool for brands looking to tap into engaged communities. Influencers have established credibility with their audience, making their endorsements highly valuable. Here's how to build successful influencer collaborations:

- **Identify the Right Influencers** – Look for influencers whose audience aligns with your target market. Micro-influencers (10k-100k followers) often have higher engagement rates than mega-influencers.
- **Establish Clear Goals** – Determine whether you want to drive brand awareness, increase conversions, or grow your social media following.
- **Choose the Right Collaboration Model** – Options include sponsored posts, product gifting, affiliate partnerships, or long-term brand ambassadorships.
- **Negotiate Compensation & Deliverables** – Payment can be monetary or product-based, depending on the influencer's reach and engagement.
- **Encourage Creative Freedom** – Influencers know their audience best; allow them to present your brand in an authentic and engaging way.

- **Monitor Performance** – Use tracking links, unique promo codes, and engagement metrics to measure campaign success.

A strong influencer partnership can drive traffic, increase brand loyalty, and provide authentic engagement that traditional ads may struggle to achieve.

Measuring ROI on Paid & Influencer Marketing Efforts

To ensure paid advertising and influencer campaigns are effective, businesses must track and measure their ROI. Here's how:

- **Set Key Performance Metrics** – Metrics may include conversion rate, engagement rate, cost-per-acquisition (CPA), and return on ad spend (ROAS).
- **Use Tracking Tools** – Google Analytics, Facebook Ads Manager, and influencer tracking platforms can help measure campaign effectiveness.
- **Compare Organic vs. Paid Performance** – Determine if paid efforts are delivering better results than organic growth strategies.
- **Evaluate Long-Term Impact** – Brand awareness and customer retention should also be considered when assessing ROI.
- **Optimize Future Campaigns** – Use data insights to refine strategies, adjust budgets, and focus on high-performing content.

By continuously evaluating campaign performance, brands can ensure their paid advertising and influencer collaborations drive meaningful business growth.

By leveraging paid advertising and influencer collaborations, you can accelerate your brand's growth, reach targeted audiences with precision, and maximize engagement like never before. However, managing multiple campaigns, tracking engagement, and maintaining consistency across platforms can be overwhelming without the right tools. That's where social media management and automation tools come in. In the next chapter, we'll explore how to streamline your workflow, automate repetitive tasks, and ensure that your social media presence remains active and impactful—without consuming all of your time.

Activity: Launch & Analyze

To help reinforce the key lessons from this chapter, apply what you've learned by running a small-scale paid ad or setting up an influencer collaboration. Choose one of the following activities:

Option 1: Run a Paid Ad Experiment

- Set aside a budget of $20-$30 for a test ad.
- Choose a platform (e.g. Facebook, Instagram, TikTok or LinkedIn) based on your audience .
- Decide on a goal (e.g. increase engagement, drive website traffic, or promote a product.
- Determine your ad format (e.g. an image, video, or carousel ad) —keep it visually appealing.
- Select the demographic and interest-based targeting or let the platform find similar users.
- Run A/B Testing of the ad with different headlines, images, or calls to action.
- Let the ad run for 3-5 days, then analyze engagement, cost-per-click, and conversions.
- Reflect on "What worked best?" "What could be improved?" and "Did your targeting align with your expected results?"

Option 2: Secure an Influencer Collaboration

- Identify a micro-influencer (10K-100K followers) in your niche.
- Send a collaboration proposal—offer a free product/service in exchange for a shoutout, or negotiate a paid partnership.
- Decide if the influencer will create a review, tutorial, unboxing, or live Q&A about your brand.
- Use promo codes, affiliate links, or engagement metrics to measure success.
- Reflect on "How did their audience respond?" "What type of content generated the most engagement?" and "Would you collaborate with them again?

Chapter 7: Social Media Management Tools & Automation

Managing social media effectively requires efficiency, consistency, and the ability to analyze and adapt quickly. As businesses and brands expand their digital presence, using the right tools and automation techniques can make a significant difference in optimizing workflow and maintaining engagement. Social media management tools help schedule content, track analytics, and streamline engagement, while automation ensures repetitive tasks don't consume valuable time. However, automation must be implemented strategically to maintain authenticity and a personalized connection with audiences. This chapter will explore the best scheduling and management tools, discuss automation strategies, and highlight the role of AI in modern social media management.

Scheduling and Management Tools

Full transparency moment: I have not used all of these tools, so you will have to experiment with them and find the one that works best for you. However, I have used four out of the eight (Hootsuite, Buffer, Sprout Social, and Radian6). There are several tools available to help businesses manage their social media presence effectively. Some of the most widely used include:

- **Hootsuite** – One of the most comprehensive social media management tools, Hootsuite allows users to schedule posts across multiple platforms, monitor mentions and engagement, and access detailed analytics.
- **Buffer** – Known for its simplicity and ease of use, Buffer helps schedule posts, track performance, and collaborate with teams on social media strategies.
- **Sprout Social** – A robust tool offering social media scheduling, analytics, and customer engagement features, making it a great choice for businesses looking to streamline operations.

- **Radian6** – A monitoring and analytics tool that helps businesses track brand mentions, analyze sentiment, and engage with audiences in real time to optimize their social media strategy.
- **Later** – Focused on visual content, Later is ideal for Instagram scheduling, offering a visual planner that helps brands create cohesive feeds.
- **CoSchedule** – An excellent tool for content marketers, allowing integration with blogs and social media for a more synchronized content calendar.
- **Agorapulse** – Combines social media scheduling, reporting, and team collaboration features, along with a strong focus on audience engagement.
- **SocialBee** – Helps businesses categorize content, ensuring a diverse mix of posts while automating publishing.

Each tool has its strengths, and selecting the right one depends on your brand's needs, budget, and required functionality.

Automating Repetitive Tasks Without Losing Authenticity

Automation in social media management can save time and increase efficiency, but it must be implemented carefully to maintain a brand's unique voice and engagement. Here's how to balance automation with authenticity:

- **Automate Scheduling but Maintain Real-Time Interaction** – Use tools to schedule posts in advance but stay active by responding to comments and engaging with trending topics in real-time.
- **Use Chatbots for Initial Responses** – Automated chatbots can provide quick replies to frequently asked questions but should allow seamless transitions to human interactions for more complex inquiries.
- **Batch Content Creation but Personalize Messaging** – While bulk content creation helps maintain consistency, adding personalized captions and tailored messaging ensures authenticity.

- **Leverage Auto-Posting but Adapt to Current Events** – Automated posting keeps social media active, but brands should be ready to adjust messaging based on trending topics and world events.
- **Monitor and Adjust Automated Responses** – Avoid robotic-sounding interactions by tweaking chatbot responses to sound more natural and brand-specific.
- **Analyze Automated Engagement Patterns** – Review automated interactions and adjust messaging to align with audience preferences and feedback.

By combining automation with human interaction, brands can maintain efficiency while ensuring genuine connections with their audience.

The Role of AI in Social Media Management

Artificial intelligence (AI) is revolutionizing social media management by enhancing personalization, improving efficiency, and providing deep insights into audience behavior. Here's how AI is shaping the future of social media:

- **AI-Powered Content Creation** – AI-driven tools like ChatGPT and Jasper can generate captions, blog posts, and even social media graphics, reducing the time needed for content creation.
- **Predictive Analytics** – AI analyzes past performance and audience behavior to predict the best times to post, which types of content will perform well, and how users will interact with posts.
- **Sentiment Analysis** – AI-powered tools can scan comments and mentions to determine audience sentiment, helping brands respond appropriately to feedback.
- **Advanced Audience Targeting** – AI algorithms enhance ad targeting by analyzing user data and creating highly personalized marketing campaigns.
- **Smart Chatbots** – AI-driven chatbots provide more intuitive customer service by understanding context and

sentiment, offering personalized responses rather than generic replies.

- **Automated Image & Video Recognition** – AI can analyze visual content, helping brands track brand mentions even when users don't tag them directly.
- **Fraud Detection & Fake Engagement Filtering** – AI helps detect and remove fake followers and engagement, ensuring brands work with authentic audiences.

AI is becoming an essential part of social media management, but it should be used alongside human creativity and strategic thinking to maintain genuine connections with audiences.

By leveraging social media management and automation tools, you can streamline your workflow, maintain consistency, and free up valuable time while still keeping your audience engaged. From scheduling content to monitoring performance and automating repetitive tasks, these tools are essential for maintaining an efficient and impactful social media presence. However, while automation enhances productivity, it's equally important to balance efficiency with authentic engagement—because at the end of the day, social media is about building real connections.

But what happens when things don't go as planned? Social media can be unpredictable, and crises can arise at any time—whether it's negative feedback, misinformation, or a PR disaster. That's why crisis management and reputation building are critical aspects of any successful social media strategy. In the next chapter, we'll explore how to handle negative comments, navigate PR crises, protect your brand's online reputation, and, yes, we'll talk about what to do with those trolls and bots.

Chapter 8: Crisis Management & Reputation Building

For eight years, while serving in the United States Air Force, it was my job to manage crises. I became so proficient at this that I developed crisis resilience—the ability to remain calm, composed, and strategic in high-pressure situations. Although your business may not be dealing with medical evacuations, in-flight emergencies, bomb threats, or suicides, it is critical to have a plan for how your company or brand will respond to an online crisis.

In 2019, just months before the COVID-19 pandemic, I started a new role with a medical association. I don't have to remind you of the fiascos that unfolded during that time or the sheer volume of misinformation flooding social media feeds. However, for medical professionals, it was a nightmare. False claims ranged from drinking bleach to cure COVID-19 to vaccines containing microchips, and my personal favorite—the myth that Black people couldn't get COVID-19. Speaking as a Black man... I got COVID twice.

Trying to combat misinformation at the rate it was spreading would have been impossible without a crisis communications plan. Having a structured approach not only helps determine what warrants a response but also ensures that critical components are in place to deliver a strong and efficient reaction to misinformation and crises.

In today's ever-evolving digital landscape, a brand's online reputation is one of its most valuable assets. Social media has the power to build brands, but it can also amplify crises in a matter of minutes. Negative comments, PR crises, misinformation, and online trolls can significantly impact public perception. The way a brand responds to these challenges can either enhance or damage its credibility.

In this chapter, we will explore proven strategies for handling negative comments and PR crises, maintaining a positive brand image, and dealing with social media trolls and misinformation. By implementing a proactive crisis management plan, businesses can navigate challenges effectively while strengthening their brand reputation.

Handling Negative Comments and PR Crises

Negative comments and public relations crises are inevitable in today's digital world. Whether it's an unhappy customer, a viral complaint, or a misstep by a brand, the way a business responds is crucial.

Here are five steps to include in your crisis comm plan:

1. **Acknowledge and Assess** – The first step in managing negativity is acknowledging the issue. Ignoring it can make matters worse. Assess whether the complaint is valid or if it's an attempt to stir controversy.
2. **Respond Quickly and Professionally** – Timeliness matters in crisis management. Responding promptly shows accountability and a willingness to resolve issues. Maintain a professional, empathetic, and respectful tone.
3. **Take the Conversation Offline** – If possible, resolve issues privately by directing the conversation to direct messages, email, or a customer service helpline.
4. **Apologize When Necessary** – If the brand is at fault, a genuine apology goes a long way in diffusing tension. Transparency fosters trust and loyalty.
5. **Monitor and Adapt** – Use social listening tools to track conversations and sentiment about your brand. Learning from past mistakes helps refine communication strategies.

By implementing these steps, businesses can turn negative situations into opportunities to demonstrate their commitment to customer satisfaction and brand integrity.

Strategies for Maintaining a Positive Brand Image

A positive brand image is built over time through consistent actions, messaging, and customer experiences. Here are some strategies to maintain and enhance your brand's reputation:

- **Deliver Consistently High-Quality Content** – Share valuable, insightful, and relevant content that resonates with your audience.
- **Engage Authentically** – Respond to comments, messages, and mentions with a personal and genuine approach.
- **Showcase Positive Customer Stories** – Highlight testimonials, reviews, and user-generated content that demonstrate positive brand experiences.
- **Align with Social Responsibility** – Supporting meaningful causes and practicing corporate social responsibility strengthens brand credibility.
- **Build Trust Through Transparency** – Address mistakes openly and communicate updates on improvements.
- **Train Your Team** – Ensure employees understand brand values and crisis communication protocols to maintain a unified voice.

Maintaining a positive brand image requires consistency, honesty, and engagement. A well-managed reputation leads to greater brand loyalty and trust.

Dealing with Social Media Trolls and Misinformation

Trolls and misinformation can disrupt a brand's online presence and credibility. Here's how to handle them effectively:

- **Recognize Troll Behavior** – Trolls seek to provoke reactions rather than engage in constructive discussions. Recognizing their intent helps brands determine the best course of action.
- **Avoid Feeding the Trolls** – Engaging with trolls often escalates conflicts. If a comment is clearly meant to incite, it's best to ignore or hide it.
- **Moderate Comments and Implement Community Guidelines** – Establish clear guidelines for your social media pages, outlining acceptable behavior and enforcing moderation policies.

- **Correct Misinformation Promptly** – If false information spreads about your brand, address it with factual and well-sourced responses.
- **Leverage Brand Advocates** – A strong community of loyal followers often defends the brand against trolls and misinformation, making brand advocacy a valuable asset.
- **Utilize Reporting Tools** – Most social media platforms allow reporting of abusive or misleading content. Use these tools to maintain a safe and credible space.

Tackling trolls and misinformation effectively ensures that your brand remains a trusted and respected presence in the digital landscape.

In an effort to increase participation for an annual medical meeting, the medical association I was working for invited a well-known guest speaker. However, once we announced the speaker, there was immediate backlash from our audience. Instead of ignoring the criticism, we took swift action—we issued a public statement apologizing for the oversight, acknowledged our misstep, and retracted the guest speaker from the event. The response was overwhelmingly positive—our audience applauded us for our transparency, accountability, and quick resolution.

This experience reinforced a valuable lesson: owning mistakes, taking full accountability, and being transparent can go a long way in crisis response. When handled correctly, even a potential PR disaster can strengthen trust in your brand.

Establishing a crisis management plan equips you and your team with clear guidelines for handling crises, misinformation, and online trolls. With a well-prepared approach, you can protect your brand's reputation and navigate challenges with confidence.

Now, let's shift gears and explore social media monetization strategies. In the next chapter, we'll discuss how brands and content creators can turn their online presence into profitable ventures.

Chapter 9: Monetizing Social Media

Social media is no longer just a platform for communication and engagement—it has evolved into a powerful revenue-generating tool for businesses, content creators, and entrepreneurs. Whether through affiliate marketing, sponsored content, selling digital products, or building membership communities, the potential to monetize social media is vast. However, success requires a strategic approach, authenticity, and a deep understanding of your audience's needs.

In this chapter, we will explore key monetization strategies, including affiliate marketing and sponsored content, creating and selling digital products or services, and generating revenue through memberships and subscriptions. By implementing these techniques, you can turn your social media presence into a sustainable income stream.

Affiliate Marketing and Sponsored Content

Affiliate marketing and sponsored content are two of the most accessible ways to monetize social media, allowing individuals and businesses to earn revenue by promoting products and services.

1. **Affiliate Marketing**
    - Affiliate marketing involves promoting products or services through unique tracking links and earning a commission for each sale or action generated through those links.
    - Popular affiliate networks include Amazon Associates, ShareASale, and CJ Affiliate.
    - Best practices for success:
        - ✓ Promote products relevant to your audience and niche.
        - ✓ Create authentic, high-value content that integrates affiliate links naturally.

        - ✓ Use multiple platforms, such as blogs, YouTube, and Instagram, to increase conversions.

2. **Sponsored Content**
    - Sponsored content involves collaborating with brands to create content that highlights their products or services in exchange for compensation.
    - Factors that influence sponsorship rates include follower count, engagement rate, and niche relevance.
    - Best practices for success:
        - ✓ Partner with brands that align with your values and audience interests.
        - ✓ Disclose sponsorships transparently to maintain audience trust.
        - ✓ Create compelling content that provides value beyond simple promotion.

Affiliate marketing and sponsored content work best when combined with a strong personal brand and an engaged audience. Authenticity is key—followers are more likely to engage with content that feels genuine rather than overly promotional.

Creating and Selling Digital Products/Services

Selling digital products and services is one of the most lucrative ways to monetize social media. Unlike physical products, digital products require minimal overhead and can be sold repeatedly without additional costs.

1. **Types of Digital Products**
    - E-books and guides
    - Online courses and webinars
    - Digital templates and printables
    - Exclusive stock photos or design elements
2. **Developing and Selling Digital Services**
    - Social media consulting and coaching
    - Graphic design, video editing, and branding services

    - Copywriting, SEO services, and digital marketing
3. **Best Practices for Success**
    - Identify audience pain points and create products that provide solutions.
    - Use social media to market and showcase the value of your offerings.
    - Automate sales using platforms like Gumroad, Teachable, or Etsy.

Digital products and services provide scalable revenue opportunities, making them an excellent long-term monetization strategy for individuals and businesses alike.

Generating Revenue Through Memberships and Subscriptions

Membership and subscription-based models provide a recurring income stream, allowing brands and creators to monetize exclusive content and community engagement.

1. **Types of Membership & Subscription Models**
    - Private Facebook groups or Discord communities
    - Patreon-style memberships with tiered benefits
    - Subscription-based content on platforms like YouTube and Substack
2. **Benefits of Membership Models**
    - Predictable, recurring revenue stream
    - Deeper community engagement and brand loyalty
    - Opportunities for premium content and services
3. **Best Practices for Success**
    - Offer exclusive value that members can't get elsewhere.
    - Foster an engaged community by interacting with members regularly.
    - Provide incentives such as early access, exclusive content, or direct Q&A sessions.

By leveraging memberships and subscription-based models, businesses and content creators can build sustainable income streams while deepening their relationship with their audience.

As social media continues to evolve, so do the opportunities for monetization. The key to long-term success lies in diversifying revenue streams—leveraging affiliate marketing, digital products, and memberships to create a stable, scalable, and sustainable income. By tapping into multiple monetization strategies, you can maximize your earning potential, expand your reach, and build a thriving online presence that generates consistent revenue.

Final Thoughts

The ultimate success in social media management lies in understanding the ever-evolving landscape of digital engagement and strategically leveraging it to meet business goals. Throughout this guide, several key principles emerged that emphasized the importance of a thoughtful, data-driven approach to social media. These concepts apply to businesses of all sizes, from solopreneurs to multinational corporations, highlighting that no one can afford to overlook the critical role social media plays in today's marketing and customer engagement strategies.

The first, and perhaps most crucial takeaway, is the importance of creating a robust social media strategy. Without a clear and actionable plan, social media efforts often become fragmented and ineffective. A solid strategy starts with defining clear goals — whether they be brand awareness, lead generation, or customer engagement. From there, businesses need to identify their target audience and understand their needs, habits, and preferences. Armed with this knowledge, businesses can craft content that resonates deeply, using the right tone, format, and timing to achieve their desired results.

I emphasize that flexibility is key. While a strategy should guide actions, it's essential to remain adaptable to new trends, platform updates, or shifts in audience behavior. This adaptability enables businesses to stay relevant in a constantly changing digital environment.

Content is the heart of social media, and creating the right kind of content is essential to any successful strategy. Whether it's blogs, articles, videos, infographics, or memes, content must align with both audience preferences and business objectives. Visual storytelling, in particular, plays a critical role in capturing attention, especially on image-heavy platforms like Instagram and Pinterest. Therefore, businesses should prioritize the creation of compelling visual content alongside written posts.

Another key theme in this guide is the importance of engagement. Posting content isn't enough — social media is inherently interactive, and active engagement with followers is crucial for building community and trust. Responding to comments, answering questions, and participating in conversations helps humanize brands, fostering lasting relationships with audiences. This interaction breeds loyalty and makes customers feel valued, encouraging them to continue supporting the brand.

No social media strategy is complete without an understanding of performance metrics. I highlighted the value of tracking and analyzing data to assess the effectiveness of social media campaigns. Metrics like reach, engagement, click-through rates, and conversions provide valuable insights into what works and what doesn't. By consistently reviewing these analytics, businesses can optimize their social media efforts and make adjustments to improve results over time.

Data-driven decision-making is a hallmark of the most successful social media managers. Through A/B testing, businesses can refine their messaging and strategies, ensuring that they continually move closer to their desired outcomes. The ability to pivot quickly based on analytical insights ensures that resources are maximized and social media ROI is optimized.

Selecting the right social media platforms is crucial. While numerous platforms are available, not all may be appropriate for every business. Understanding where your target audience spends their time is essential. For example, Instagram and TikTok are ideal for brands targeting younger audiences with visual content, while LinkedIn is better suited for B2B businesses looking to connect with professionals.

Focusing efforts on a few key platforms, rather than spreading oneself too thin across multiple sites, ensures greater effectiveness. This targeted approach allows for deeper engagement with audiences and enables businesses to optimize their presence on the platforms that matter most. It also simplifies content creation, as businesses can tailor messaging and media formats to the specific requirements of each platform.

As businesses grow, managing social media becomes increasingly complex. For larger organizations, establishing a dedicated social media team with clearly defined roles is highly recommended. These roles may include content creators, community managers, data analysts, and strategists. Effective communication and coordination within the team are vital to ensure that all social media activities align with the broader marketing strategy.

We also discussed the importance of using the right social media management tools. These tools help streamline the posting process, schedule content in advance, and track performance metrics. By saving businesses valuable time and effort, these tools enable them to maintain a consistent presence across multiple platforms while minimizing the risk of errors.

An often-overlooked aspect of social media management is crisis communication. I highlighted how social media can amplify both positive and negative feedback, making it essential for businesses to be prepared for any situation. A well-developed crisis management plan ensures that businesses can quickly and effectively respond to negative comments or reviews, minimizing potential damage to their reputation.

Having a clear protocol for handling difficult situations — whether related to customer complaints, product issues, or public relations crises — enables businesses to respond swiftly and professionally. Social media managers should be trained in de-escalation techniques and in maintaining the brand's voice during challenging times.

Finally, I stressed the importance of staying current with social media trends. The digital landscape is constantly evolving, with new features, tools, and platforms emerging regularly. Social media managers must remain informed and adaptable. Whether it's adopting new video formats like short-form TikTok videos or exploring the potential of augmented reality filters, being an early adopter can offer a competitive edge. By staying up-to-date, businesses can keep their social media presence fresh and engaging, ensuring they maintain a strong connection with their audience.

In closing, social media management is a vital component of modern marketing that requires a blend of creativity, strategy, and data analysis. The key to success lies in understanding the nuances of each platform, creating compelling content that resonates with your audience, and continuously evaluating and optimizing performance. Businesses that integrate social media management into their broader marketing efforts can build stronger relationships with their customers, increase brand visibility, and ultimately achieve their business goals.

By staying informed about trends, leveraging analytics, and engaging authentically with followers, businesses can thrive in this competitive digital space. Social media management is not just about posting content — it's about building meaningful connections that lead to long-term success.

Afterword

I hope you have enjoyed reading this book, but more importantly, I hope you've gained valuable insights from the pages within. Throughout my nearly 30-year career in communications and marketing, I've learned far more than I could ever teach in a lifetime. This journey has provided me with life lessons that transcend business and branding, offering deeper understandings of what it means to connect genuinely with others.

If you found this book helpful, I encourage you to share it by leaving a review and passing it along to your team or someone you know in the field. They will be grateful, and I will be even more appreciative than I am now.

Thank you for taking the time to read this book. My deepest gratitude and heartfelt appreciation go out to you.

Kenneth Spresley

www.ingramcontent.com/pod-product-compliance
Lightning Source LLC
LaVergne TN
LVHW050939210926
848482LV00013B/674